Careers in ENGINEERING

A Career In Biomedical Engineering

Other titles in the *Careers in Engineering* series include:

A Career in Civil Engineering

A Career in Computer Engineering

A Career in Electrical Engineering

A Career in Environmental Engineering

A Career in Mechanical Engineering

Careers in
ENGINEERING

A Career In Biomedical Engineering

Melissa Abramovitz

ReferencePoint Press®

San Diego, CA

© 2019 ReferencePoint Press, Inc.
Printed in the United States

For more information, contact:
ReferencePoint Press, Inc.
PO Box 27779
San Diego, CA 92198
www.ReferencePointPress.com

LIBRARY OF CONGRESS CATALOGING-IN-PUBLICATION DATA

Names: Abramovitz, Melissa, 1954– author.
Title: A Career in Biomedical Engineering/by Melissa Abramovitz.
Description: San Diego, CA: ReferencePoint Press, Inc., [2018] | Series: Careers in Engineering | Audience: Grades 9 to 12. | Includes bibliographical references and index.
Identifiers: LCCN 2017060396 (print) | LCCN 2018005880 (ebook) | ISBN 9781682823446 (eBook) | ISBN 9781682823439 (hardback)
Subjects: LCSH: Biomedical engineering—Vocational guidance—Juvenile literature. | Biomedical engineers—Juvenile literature. | Vocational guidance.
Classification: LCC R856.2 (ebook) | LCC R856.2 .A27 2018 (print) | DDC 610.28—dc23
LC record available at https://lccn.loc.gov/2017060396

CONTENTS

BIOMEDICAL ENGINEER AT A GLANCE

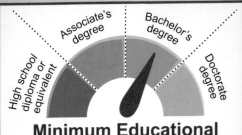

Minimum Educational Requirements

High school diploma or equivalent

Associate's degree

Bachelor's degree

Doctorate degree

Working Conditions

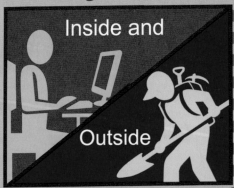

Inside and

Outside

Personal Qualities

- ☑ Analytical, math, and problem-solving skills
- ☑ Communication skills
- ☑ Creativity
- ☑ High ethical standards
- ☑ A desire to help others

Median Pay in 2016 — $85,620

21,300
Number of jobs as of 2016

Growth rate through 2026
7%

Future Job Outlook

Source: Bureau of Labor Statistics, *Occupational Outlook Handbook*. www.bls.gov.

A Growing Engineering Field

Biomedical engineers work in one of the fastest-growing engineering fields. Their work involves using principles of engineering and biology to design and create devices, drugs, and other products and technologies that improve health care. While biomedical engineering is a fairly new engineering discipline, biomedical engineers do the same types of things that other engineers have done for thousands of years. The International Federation of Consulting Engineers defines engineers as "problem solvers, organisers, calculators and designers. They are capable of clearly defining a problem and its relevant constraints (such as time, cost, etc.) and providing a simple solution. They are always seeking quicker, better, and less expensive ways to improve quality of life for everyone."[1]

Types of Engineers

There are many types of engineers, including aerospace, materials, mechanical, chemical, and computer engineers. Engineering professional societies describe more than twenty-five specialized engineering fields. Each field contains subfields. For instance, subfields of biomedical engineering include biomedical materials engineering, biomedical imaging engineering, genetic engineering, and stem cell engineering.

Engineers in diverse fields and subfields create everyday items like vehicles, engines, computers, bridges, roads, and systems that bring water to homes. They also turn ideas that were once in the realm of science fiction into reality by inventing products like space suits and thought-controlled computers. Biomedical engineers are especially known for transforming science fiction into reality. For instance, biomedical engineers at the BioBots company invented a new type of 3-D printer that quickly creates artificial skin or bones to replace damaged tissue. When this machine became available in 2015, it brought futuristic ideas like the Replicator (seen in the *Star Trek* television shows and movies) into real life. The Replicator fabricated food, tools, and other items from computer-based instructions.

The Biomedical Engineering Discipline

Biomedical engineers have made hundreds of other science fiction–like ideas real, and the field's relative newness as a formal engineering discipline makes these rapid advances all the more remarkable. Indeed, biomedical engineering is the only engineering branch that became a formal engineering discipline after World War II (1939–1945). Its comparatively recent emergence stems from the fact that most people did not think engineering had anything to do with biology and health throughout most of history. Instead, most doctors and laypeople thought disease was caused by supernatural forces, and most healers focused on driving out evil spirits rather than seeking scientifically engineered solutions. But this started to change in the 1600s, when physicians began to realize that principles of physics, chemistry, and engineering apply to human health and illness. In 1628 the British physician William Harvey was one of the first to propose that living beings function according to principles of physics. Harvey described the heart, for instance, as a machine that pumps blood.

Applying principles of science and engineering to living beings became even more prevalent during the nineteenth and twentieth centuries. For example, in 1895 the German mechanical engineer Wilhelm Roentgen discovered X-rays, and doctors began using X-ray machines to view bones inside the human body. This kickstarted the field of medical imagery. Another event that helped unify engineering and medicine occurred in the 1950s, when the American biologist James Watson and the British physicist Francis Crick discovered the structure of the DNA molecule, paving the way for genetic engineering.

These innovations and numerous other new biomedical technologies that emerged in the mid-1900s led to the recognition of biomedical engineering as a formal engineering discipline in the late 1960s. Around that time the first biomedical engineering departments opened at the University of Virginia, Case Western Reserve University, Johns Hopkins University, and Duke University. Since then many colleges and universities have added biomedical engineering, bioengineering, and similar departments. These terms are sometimes used interchangeably, but often *bioengineering* applies to any use of biological systems, including in agriculture and energy production, while *biomedical engineering* applies only to health care. In 2000, when the National Institutes of Health established the National Institute of Biomedical Imaging and Bioengineering (NIBIB) to enhance research efforts in these fields, the status of biomedical

> "Anyone interested in biomedical engineering will certainly find a very specific field that interests them while still being able to cross over to other fields with relative ease."[3]
>
> —National Human Genome Research Institute

engineering and bioengineering as independent disciplines became even more firmly entrenched. The NIBIB has since funneled millions of dollars to biomedical engineering researchers, and increasing numbers of biomedical technology companies have also led to tremendous growth in relevant careers.

Limitless Opportunities

The Try Engineering website notes that any engineering degree "can provide you with access to any field, any profession, any industry, or any career you might be interested in pursuing. . . . The opportunities are limitless,"[2] because knowing how to solve real-world problems is useful in many areas. However, experts believe that earning a biomedical engineering or closely related degree is especially valuable because this "young" engineering discipline is growing to encompass more subfields all the time. According to the National Human Genome Research Institute, "Anyone interested in biomedical engineering will certainly find a very specific field that interests them while still being able to cross over to other fields with relative ease."[3]

CHAPTER 1

What Does a Biomedical Engineer Do?

Biomedical engineers use their knowledge of biology and engineering to create solutions to health care problems. As the American Institute for Medical and Biological Engineering (AIMBE) explains, "Biomedical engineers dream up creative, practical solutions and work with other smart, inspiring people to invent, design, and create things that matter—they turn ideas into reality in order to make our lives safer, more enjoyable, and more productive."[4] This may involve improving existing tools or working on specialized aspects of imagining, creating, or testing new products and technologies used in diagnosing, treating, and preventing illness or injury.

Harnessing New Technologies

Regardless of biomedical engineers' specialty, they all apply up-to-date knowledge about biology, chemistry, computer science, biomechanics, biomaterials, and other science and engineering disciplines to create products that meet specific needs. Prior to the 1970s, for example, surgeons had to surgically open a patient's chest or abdomen to diagnose diseases of the digestive system. But biomedical engineers who create diagnostic instruments responded to doctors' pleas for new devices that would let them view people's insides without cutting the body open. Starting in the late 1960s, these engineers devised methods of incorporating advances in fiber optics—the use of glass fibers to transmit images—and in miniaturized cameras to create the endoscope. An endoscope consists of an eyepiece on one end of a flexible tube and a miniature camera on the other end. Doctors guide the tube through a patient's mouth into the esophagus and stomach. They can see and photograph the insides of these areas.

Biomedical engineers improved endoscopes as other technological advances occurred. In the late 1970s, new digital imaging technologies allowed engineers to create endoscopes that send images recorded by the camera to a computer for analysis. Later on, technologies used to create high-definition images in televisions were incorporated into endoscopes to make it easier for doctors to identify internal abnormalities. But as gastrointestinal specialist Dr. Michael Sivak points out, "Progress occurred largely through incorporation of technologies from other fields. Most of our technology was not, in fact, invented specifically for endoscopy."[5]

However, in some cases incorporating existing technologies or products into biomedical devices does not work well. For instance, the first artificial hearts made in the mid-1900s were constructed from polyether urethanes, a type of plastic used in women's girdles, because these materials could stretch. But these substances did not function well within a living body, and patients experienced many complications like blood clots. Problems with these and other materials used in implantable technologies led biomedical engineers with biomaterials expertise to start creating new materials to meet specific needs. For artificial hearts, using materials made by combining various compounds with a metal called titanium proved to give much better results.

> "Biomedical engineers dream up creative, practical solutions and work with other smart, inspiring people to invent, design, and create things that matter."[4]
>
> —AIMBE

Cooperation and Collaboration

Whatever specific job biomedical engineers do, they all collaborate with other engineers, scientists, clinicians, business and marketing experts, and other specialists who may work at the same place or elsewhere. According to the University of Wisconsin–Madison Department of Biomedical Engineering website, "In most academic departments, cross-disciplinary collaboration is welcomed, but not required—considered more the professional icing than the cake. Not so for biomedical engineering, a field where researchers define themselves by their direct connections to translational medicine [applying research results directly to helping patients] and health care."[6] This is true for biomedical engineers in industry as well as in academia.

Lori Laird is a biomedical engineer who works for the Guidant Corporation in Santa Clara, California, designing, creating, and testing minimally invasive instruments for surgeons who operate on blood vessels. She collaborates with manufacturing engineers and quality control engineers at Guidant to ensure the products are safe and effective. She also interacts with doctors who contact Guidant about the need for certain products and follows up by watching and assessing surgeries in which these doctors use the products she creates.

Creating complex biomedical products sometimes involves collaboration between teams of specialized biomedical engineers from several companies or academic research laboratories. In one project, teams of biomedical engineers led by Dr. Levi Hargrove at the Rehabilitation Institute of Chicago (RIC) spent several years designing, building, and testing the world's first thought-controlled bionic prosthetic (artificial) leg. Amputee Zac Vawter then spent three years helping the team tweak the mechanics and computer systems that run the device before it was introduced to the world in 2012. At that time, Vawter used the leg to climb 103 flights of stairs to the top of the Willis Tower in Chicago.

Biomaterials and biomechanics experts at Vanderbilt University and at a company called Freedom Innovations created materials that made the prosthetic as lightweight and sturdy as possible. They also created a unique system of sensors, motors, belts, and chains. These moving parts were designed to respond

> "In most academic departments, cross-disciplinary collaboration is welcomed, but not required . . . Not so for biomedical engineering, a field where researchers define themselves by their direct connections to translational medicine and health care."[6]
>
> —University of Wisconsin–Madison Department of Biomedical Engineering Website

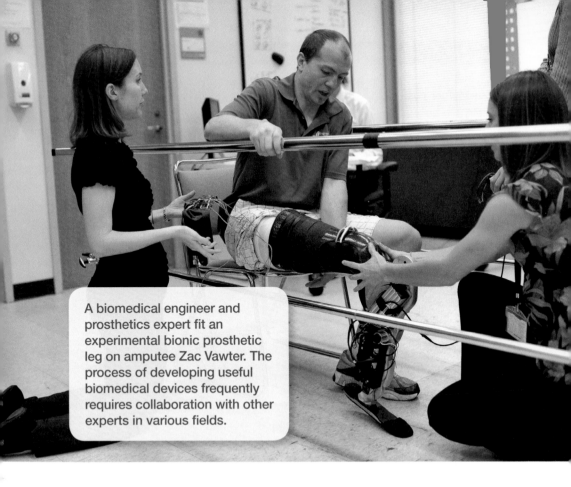

A biomedical engineer and prosthetics expert fit an experimental bionic prosthetic leg on amputee Zac Vawter. The process of developing useful biomedical devices frequently requires collaboration with other experts in various fields.

to commands from a computer that was designed and built by a team of bioinformatics specialists (biomedical engineers who use computer science, biology, and mathematics to analyze and explain biomedical data). These specialists also created software that translates instructions from the prosthetic user's brain into these commands. If Vawter thought "climb stairs," for example, the computer software translated this into commands that made the prosthetic leg climb stairs. The computer could receive input from Vawter's brain because surgeons performed an operation called targeted muscle reinnervation (TMR) on the remainder of Vawter's amputated leg. Biomedical engineer and surgeon Todd Kuiken at the RIC invented TMR for this purpose. It allows surgeons to rewire nerves that once controlled an amputated limb, so the nerves send signals from the user's brain to sensors placed in muscles near the prosthesis. The sensors then send these signals to the prosthetic's computer.

Inventing Machines That Create Biomedical Products

Biomedical engineers do not only create medical tools. Sometimes they invent machines to manufacture these tools. Graduate students Arianna McAllister and Lian Leng at the University of Toronto created the PrintAlive Bioprinter to print sheets of custom-made skin grafts for burn victims. As of late 2017, it was still being tested for safety and effectiveness.

Doctors previously expressed a need for a 3-D printer that could quickly print skin-like sheets to save burn patients' lives. Existing 3-D printers only printed hard items, not flexible structures like skin. One challenge McAllister and Leng faced was that natural skin consists of layers of two types of cells called fibroblasts and keratinocytes. Each cell type must be enveloped in a different type of liquid to stay alive.

The researchers overcame this challenge by designing a print cartridge with separate channels for each type of cell and liquid. Each cell/liquid mixture is squirted from its channel into a container holding another liquid that turns it into a gel-like material. The printer then prints a layer of keratinocytes and a layer of fibroblasts at the same time, merging both mixtures into a skin-like sheet McAllister and Leng call a "living bandage."

Quoted in Mike McLeod, "3D Skin Graft Bioprinter Wins Canadian 2014 James Dyson Award," *Design Engineering*, September 18, 2014. www.design-engineering.com.

The involvement of these subspecialists brought the latest technologies to the project and contributed to what Vawter calls "a huge milestone for me and for all leg amputees,"[7] because unlike other prosthetic legs, it allowed him to move in more natural ways.

Sub-subspecialists

Biomedical engineers not only specialize in creating products in subfields such as biomechanics; each of these subfields has sub-subfields in which certain engineers specialize. For instance, some bioinformatics specialists design and use software to run biomedical equipment. Others create computer simulations of the human body or build mathematical and statistical models to help other engineers understand biological functions like heartbeats. In fact, the number of bioinformatics engineers involved has grown significantly since the first such experts emerged in the 1980s. These engineers are now classified as specialists in the fast-growing sub-subfield of computational biology.

Computational biologists use tools like algorithms, robotic models, machine learning programs, and imaging data to create computer models of biological systems. Their work impacts diverse areas of biomedical engineering, including drug design, gene sequencing, and brain science. For example, computational models can help biomedical engineers predict how certain cells, groups of cells, or complete body organs will respond to an experimental drug. This allows drug developers to discard or promote new drug ideas early on in the testing process, which saves much time and money because only those drugs that are likely to be successful are then tested in expensive clinical studies. Stanford University computer science professor Daphne Koller notes that "the challenges in [computational biology] are never-ending and there's always a need for smart people to look at the data and figure out how to extract the most information from them."[8]

Enforcing Regulations and Protecting the Public

Another specialty that biomedical engineers can pursue deals with regulatory and legal matters. Some, like Irene Bacalocostantis, evaluate medical devices and drugs for the Food and Drug Administration (FDA). Bacalocostantis works for the FDA's Center for Devices and Radiological Health as a premarket medical device reviewer. Her job is to analyze the safety and effectiveness of new medical devices used in gastroenterology (the medical specialty that deals with the digestive system) before manufacturers are permitted to sell these devices. She also develops FDA policies and guidelines for others who assess the safety and effectiveness of medical devices. She thus must be well versed in the medical conditions these devices are invented to diagnose or treat, as well as in assessing all aspects of device safety and effectiveness.

CHAPTER 2

How Do You Become a Biomedical Engineer?

People interested in a biomedical engineering career can prepare by taking certain courses in high school. Most colleges and universities recommend that aspiring biomedical engineers take four years of math and English, a year each of physics, chemistry, and biology, and the mix of social studies and languages found in most college-prep high school programs. Courses in computer programming and mechanical drawing or drafting are also useful. Since some biomedical engineers work in government agencies, experts believe being involved in student government and school policy committees in high school and college is also a good idea.

Summer Camps and More

Summer camps held throughout the United States can also provide high school students with knowledge and hands-on experience in biomedical engineering. For example, the US Naval Academy in Annapolis, Maryland, sponsors weeklong Summer STEM (science, technology, engineering, and math) camps for high school students interested in engineering careers. These camps include hands-on projects and interactions with mentors who work as engineers. One student describes the camp he attended as "helpful, fun, and exciting."[9]

The Mitre Corporation's Nanosystems Group summer program also helps high school students plan a future career. Mitre operates federally funded research centers that develop solutions to national security, health care, and other critical problems. Eliah Shamir was uncertain about her career aims before participating, but after the program taught her the necessary skills, she knew she wanted a career in biomedical engineering. The program "taught me to problem-solve, think creatively, integrate scientific disciplines, write and speak more precisely, and apply basic knowledge to help design workable devices,"[10] she says.

Internships, Co-ops, and Shadowing

Once students enter college, they can gain hands-on experience by applying for internships and cooperative education programs (co-ops) at health care facilities, government agencies, and medical device companies. Internships are paid or unpaid positions in which students work alongside professionals. Many students complete internships during the summer break from classes, but some do part-time internships when classes are in session.

Women in Engineering

Dr. Catherine Klapperich knows firsthand that becoming a biomedical engineer is more difficult for women than men because society views men as better suited for science and engineering careers. In high school Klapperich was fascinated by high-tech devices like electron microscopes, but her school counselors discouraged her from taking many science classes because she had strong writing skills. So she initially signed up for a journalism major at Northwestern University, but she eventually switched to an engineering major because that was what truly interested her. She received a bachelor's degree in materials science and engineering and went on to earn a master's degree in engineering sciences from Harvard University, followed by a PhD in mechanical engineering from the University of California–Berkeley.

Klapperich is now a professor of biomedical engineering and also teaches materials science and mechanical engineering at Boston University. She is also the director and associate dean for a NIBIB research center and the director of the Laboratory for Diagnostics and Global Healthcare Technologies. Her research focuses on developing low-cost diagnostic tests for many diseases, particularly those that affect people in impoverished areas.

The University of Arkansas Biomedical Engineering Department helped Gage Greening get an internship in 2016 at Johnson Space Center, which is part of the National Aeronautics and Space Administration (NASA). Greening worked on health screening devices for the International Space Station. "My internship was very challenging at times, but besides learning some new skills, the most important thing for me was better defining the things I want in a career,"[11] he writes.

In a co-op, students temporarily stop attending classes and work full time for three months to a year. Co-op students are paid, and many put the money toward their education costs. Some universities—including the University of Iowa, Lawrence Technological University, and the University of Virginia—require students to participate in either a co-op or internship. Besides giving students hands-on training, co-ops and internships also provide networking opportunities. Many students end up being recruited to work at the company where they did an internship or co-op.

Another type of arrangement, called shadowing, can also give students valuable insight into their future career. Shadowing involves a student spending a day or days with a professional, following him or her around to find out what he or she does. For instance, Richard Gray thought he wanted to become a physician, so he shadowed a doctor. The experience taught him that he would prefer a career with a more flexible schedule, so he decided on biomedical engineering and now works for the FDA.

> "My internship was very challenging at times, but besides learning some new skills, the most important thing for me was better defining the things I want in a career."[11]
>
> —University of Arkansas biomedical engineering student Gage Greening

College Majors for Biomedical Engineers

Internships and co-ops help students prepare to work as biomedical engineers, but earning at least a bachelor's degree is also required. Many colleges and universities offer biomedical engineering majors, but the fact that different schools use different names for these courses of study can be confusing. Sometimes

A Student's Biomedical Engineering Company

Many college undergraduates work as interns or in co-op positions at established companies, but after his junior year of college at Duke University, biomedical engineering student Sam Fox started his own company to bring his idea for a much-needed innovation to fruition. Fox found out from an occupational therapist at the Duke University health center that it is difficult for nurses and therapists to transfer hospital patients from a bed into a wheelchair. The sling-like contraptions used for this purpose make the process very slow and laborious, and caregivers and patients are easily injured.

Fox brainstormed and came up with the idea of using inflatable tubes that fit under the patient to facilitate these transfers. He entered his idea in two biomedical engineering competitions at Duke and won both. This gave him some start-up money to put toward planning further research and development of the product. His academic adviser and contacts in the school's business department generously helped him formalize his technical and business plans, and he launched his company, Zephyr Mobility, in 2017.

the terms *bioengineering*, *biological engineering*, and *biomedical engineering* are used interchangeably, but usually they refer to distinct school departments and majors. For example, Penn State offers a major in biological engineering within the Department of Agricultural and Biological Engineering, as well as a major in biomedical engineering within the Department of Biomedical Engineering. The Penn State Department of Agricultural and Biological Engineering website explains that "Biological Engineering is the application of engineering design and analysis to power and machinery systems, structures, production of food and pharmaceuticals, and protection of natural resources."[12] Biomedical engineering, in contrast, concerns "medical device design, instrumentation, medical imaging, healthcare management, biomedical research and academia,"[13] according to the Penn State Biomedical Engineering Department website.

In general, college-level biomedical engineering courses include classroom and laboratory learning about physiology, biomaterials, biochemistry, fluid and solid mechanics, computer programming, engineering design, and other engineering and biology courses. While courses that provide general knowledge about engineering and biology are valuable, Yale University professor W. Mark Saltzman notes in his textbook *Biomedical Engineering* that the growth of biomedical engineering subfields means students must focus their studies on a specialty. "Most undergraduate students majoring in biomedical engineering are faced with a decision, early in their program of study, regarding the subfield in which they would like to specialize,"[14] he writes.

> "I think the world is really opening up to women in engineering."[17]
>
> —Biomedical engineer Lori Laird of the Guidant Corporation

Students can prepare for a biomedical engineering career even if no biomedical engineering major is offered at their college or university. Most students in this position earn a bachelor of science in either chemical or mechanical engineering and take electives in biology, organic chemistry, biomechanics, and biomaterials.

Accredited Programs

Whichever degree an individual pursues, it is important to receive it from an accredited program. A nonprofit organization called the Accreditation Board for Engineering and Technology (ABET) accredits college and university programs in science and engineering. "Accreditation is proof that a collegiate program met standards essential to produce graduates ready to enter the critical fields of applied science, computing, engineering, and engineering technology,"[15] ABET explains.

ABET is affiliated with more than twenty-two hundred experts from industry, government, and academia who evaluate school programs to determine which ones meet its standards. It has accredited more than thirty-seven hundred science, engineering, and technology programs at more than 750 colleges and universities in thirty countries.

Women in Engineering

Although collegiate programs in biomedical engineering are increasingly popular, engineering majors and the profession as a whole are still male dominated. Numerous organizations that seek to increase the number of female engineers therefore offer guidance and scholarships to women who seek engineering degrees and careers. One such organization is the Society of Women Engineers. It awarded about 230 scholarships to women enrolled in accredited undergraduate or graduate engineering programs in 2016.

Other efforts focus on making engineering programs more relevant to females. For instance, biomedical engineering professor Lina Nilsson at the University of California–Berkeley writes that "women seem to be drawn to engineering projects that attempt to achieve societal good."[16] Indeed, about 50 percent of the students enrolled in her university's development engineering program are female, compared to less than 15 percent in traditional engineering programs. Development engineering students invent and design solutions to problems in low-income communities.

Since studies indicate that teachers, and society in general, still hold the idea that girls are inferior to boys in science and math, efforts to persuade more females to take STEM courses in middle and high school are also widespread. Researchers point out that toy makers still market princess dolls for girls and construction sets for boys. This is less pronounced in the twenty-first century than previously, but a 2015 study by the National Bureau of Economic Research found that elementary school teachers still encourage boys but not girls to concentrate on science and math. This bias strongly influences students' choices about enrolling in STEM classes in middle and high school.

Many women who are already biomedical engineers are especially supportive of females who choose STEM courses and pursue engineering careers, and some note that the number of women engineers is growing. "Stick with it. . . . It's going to be challenging . . . [but] I think the world is really opening up to women in engineering,"[17] states biomedical engineer Lori Laird.

CHAPTER 3

What Skills and Personal Qualities Matter Most, and Why?

The Try Engineering website defines an engineer as a "Dreamer. Innovator. Researcher. Problem Solver. Inventor. Creator."[18] This definition offers clues about some of the skills and personal qualities that are important for biomedical engineers; they must be creative and analytical and have a desire to invent products that meet certain needs. In addition, they need strong communication, computer, and math skills and must be persistent, ethical, and well versed in multiple areas of science and technology.

Why Are These Skills Important?

Creativity is important for conceiving of and inventing innovative products to meet specific needs. Indeed, engineering programs teach engineers how to use their creativity to translate a need into a new product or technology. Closely related to creativity is the need for strong analytical skills that help an engineer analyze the needs of customers and patients and use this information to create appropriate solutions. After analyzing these needs, biomedical engineers incorporate their knowledge of cutting-edge science and technology into innovative products. For instance, until the mid-1900s, the only hearing aids available to people with hearing difficulties were large, horn-shaped devices called ear trumpets. People held these unwieldly devices up to the ear to magnify sound, and many were embarrassed to use them. But after electronic engineers introduced transistors in 1948, biomedical engineers incorporated these tiny energy converters into

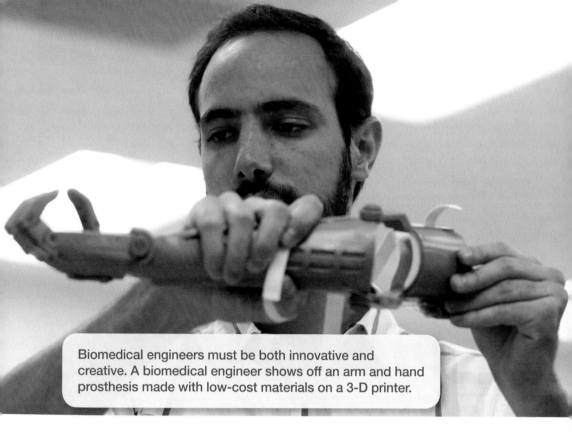

Biomedical engineers must be both innovative and creative. A biomedical engineer shows off an arm and hand prosthesis made with low-cost materials on a 3-D printer.

wearable hearing aids. Later, after miniature integrated circuits and tiny batteries were developed, engineers incorporated these technologies into even smaller hearing aids that fit inside the ear.

Strong math skills come into play because biomedical engineers use calculus, statistics, and other advanced mathematical disciplines to design and troubleshoot the products they create. Bioengineering pioneer Robert Nerem, a professor at the Georgia Institute of Technology (Georgia Tech), uses the example of research on an artificial pancreas to explain why biomedical engineers with strong math skills are better suited than regular medical researchers to develop this product, which can potentially cure type 1 diabetes. This disease results from patients' bodies destroying beta cells in the pancreas that produce insulin, a hormone that allows body cells to take in the glucose (sugar) they need to operate. The artificial pancreas will have genetically engineered cells that secrete insulin in response to certain glucose levels in the blood. "It is not enough that these cells be insulin secreting and glucose responsive," Nerem writes. "They must secrete insulin at a specific rate corresponding to the glucose concentration present in the blood. It is this quantitative genetic engineering for which we will need engineers educated to use the tools of molecular biology and who can work quantitatively."[19]

Problem-solving skills are also central to developing solutions to specific health care needs. Most biomedical engineers have enjoyed solving problems throughout their lives. Lori Laird, for example, states that she knew she wanted an engineering career because as a child she was always taking things apart and figuring out how they worked. She also enjoyed doing puzzles and solving math problems.

Persistence, Patience, and Determination

Biomedical engineering pioneer Robert Langer also enjoyed solving problems as a child. He especially liked finding out how magic tricks and chemicals in his chemistry set worked. Langer also exemplifies other important qualities for biomedical engineers— perseverance, patience, and an unwavering belief in one's dreams. Langer encountered many struggles and setbacks after earning his bachelor's degree in chemical engineering from Cornell University in 1970 and his doctorate from the Massachusetts Institute of Technology (MIT) in 1974. He applied to teach and do research at many colleges but was turned down because his ideas about applying chemical engineering to biomedicine were unconventional. "People didn't believe in my ideas; they didn't think this type of work was possible,"[20] he states. But he never gave up, and finally Dr. Judah Folkman at Boston Children's Hospital hired him to develop ways of stopping cancer cells from forming the blood vessels that allow them to thrive. While working in Folkman's laboratory, Langer developed new ideas about drug delivery systems and about using stem cells to create artificial organs. "Despite the challenges I faced, I believed these were big ideas that could change the future and help people clinically; the potential was too great to abandon these plans,"[21] he says. Langer was finally hired to teach and do biomedical research at MIT in 1978. Since then, he has obtained more than one thousand patents and won hundreds of awards for his biomedical innovations.

The Rewards of Helping Others

Wilson Greatbatch was an electrical engineer who taught and did research at the University of Buffalo in the 1950s. Yet his greatest satisfaction came from his foray into biomedical engineering. He invented the first implantable electronic pacemaker to regulate the heartbeat of people with heartbeat abnormalities.

A conversation in 1951 with two surgeons about a disease called heart block piqued Greatbatch's interest. Heart block causes an irregular heartbeat because electrical signals from the heart's upper chambers fail to reach the lower chambers. Greatbatch knew he could fix what amounted to a blocked communication signal.

He spent years tinkering with pacemaker models in his barn workshop at home and was overjoyed when one of his prototypes controlled a dog's heartbeat. "I seriously doubt if anything I ever do will ever give me the elation I felt that day when my own two cubic inch piece of electronic design controlled a living heart," he wrote in his diary.

In 1960 Greatbatch and surgeon William Chardack tested the workable model on heart patients who were close to death. One patient lived an additional eighteen months; another lived an additional thirty years. Since then, pacemakers have saved hundreds of thousands of lives.

Quoted in John Adam, "Innovative Lives: Making Hearts Beat: Wilson Greatbatch," Smithsonian Institution, February 5, 1999. http://invention.si.edu.

Elias Quijano is another example of how persistence can pay off. He grew up in a low-income immigrant neighborhood where science and engineering professions did not exist. However, he enjoyed science and math classes in high school and knew that he wanted to help others. He worked hard and gained admission to Yale University, but at first he felt overwhelmed and ill prepared compared to other students. Then he took an introductory biomedical engineering class taught by Dr. W. Mark Saltzman. Saltzman made difficult concepts easy to understand, and Quijano decided he wanted to do research that enhanced health care. His determination motivated professors to believe in him and help him pursue the research that fascinated him. He started publishing his studies on drug delivery systems and presenting the results at professional conferences while he was still an undergraduate, and he hopes his achievements will motivate others to overcome obstacles. "One day, I too hope to help students pursue research and medicine, even if it is something they never thought possible,"[22] he states.

Collaboration and a Desire to Help

Because biomedical engineers work in teams and interact with scientists, engineers, patients, and medical personnel, they also need good communication skills to clearly express themselves and to incorporate others' input into their creations. Many times, biomedical engineers also serve as the link that unites a diverse team of experts, since they understand "the language of both engineering and medicine,"[23] according to the Indiana University–Purdue University Indianapolis Engineering Department website.

Another trait that biomedical engineers share is a genuine desire to help others. Laird, for instance, states that what she likes most about being a biomedical engineer is that "you're saving someone's life."[24] Tom Chau, who initially worked for IBM as a systems design engineer, even changed jobs because of his desire to help others. The IBM job paid well and was intellectually stimulating, but Chau missed enriching hospital patients' lives like he did as a child, when he and his siblings volunteered at the hospital where their mother worked. So he began working at the Holland Bloorview Kids Rehabilitation Hospital in Toronto, Canada, inventing assistive devices for disabled children. "At the end of the day, you can see that your efforts are really having an impact on peoples' lives. Not 10 or 15 years down the road, but now,"[25] Chau states.

"At the end of the day, you can see that your efforts are really having an impact on peoples' lives. Not 10 or 15 years down the road, but now."[25]

—Biomedical engineer Tom Chau of the Holland Bloorview Kids Rehabilitation Hospital

Ethics and Honesty

Another important quality for biomedical engineers is that they are ethical and honest. They are, in fact, required to adhere to the code of ethics formulated by the Biomedical Engineering Society. The major points in this code specify that biomedical engineers shall "use their knowledge, skills, and abilities to enhance the safety, health, and welfare of the public . . . regard responsibility toward and rights of patients, including those of confidentiality and privacy, as their primary concern . . . consider the larger consequences of their work in regard to cost, availability, and delivery of health care."[26]

Ethics are especially important because medical products and procedures can harm or even kill people, so biomedical engineers follow ethical standards and avoid conflicts of interest. Conflicts of interest arise when researchers or clinicians have a financial stake in a product or procedure and allow the potential for huge profits to overshadow their ethical obligations. According to bioethicist Josephine Johnston of the Hastings Center, which studies biomedical ethics, conflicts of interest occur because university researchers often sell pharmaceutical or biomedical engineering companies the rights to their discoveries. "Studies of academic biomedical researchers have found troubling correlations between financial relationships with industry and problems with research, including a tendency to produce pro-sponsor results, increased secrecy, and study design,"[27] Johnston writes. University researchers with conflicts of interest have sometimes fabricated data or not published research results that could prevent a new product from being approved.

> "Studies of academic biomedical researchers have found troubling correlations between financial relationships with industry and problems with research, including a tendency to produce pro-sponsor results, increased secrecy, and study design."[27]
>
> —Bioethicist Josephine Johnston of the Hastings Center

A tragedy that occurred in 1999 highlights the dangers of conflicts of interest. Nineteen-year-old Jesse Gelsinger died while undergoing an experimental gene therapy procedure at the

Ethical Dilemmas in Biomedical Engineering

Ethical dilemmas affect biomedical engineers every day. For instance, a biomedical engineer at the Biotech company was offered a lot of money from a corporation that wanted to buy the rights to use a bionic prosthetic for people with no medical need who simply wanted to enhance their athletic abilities. Biomedical engineering student Daniel Fulmer examined this issue in an article he wrote for the University of Pittsburgh in 2015. He wrote:

> If I was the engineer in this situation, I would decide against selling the technology. Although it would be a very profitable way to go, it goes against the National Society of Professional Engineers' code of ethics. It states that "engineers shall not promote their own interest at the expense of the dignity and integrity of the profession" and "shall not be influenced in their professional duties by conflicting interests."

> Fulmer concluded that selling the technology would promote the engineer's self-interest and would also harm patients who could benefit from the technology. This harm would occur because demand for the product from people who just wanted to enhance their athletic abilities would raise its price, and this could leave patients who really needed it unable to afford it.

Daniel Fulmer, "Ethics in Biomedical Engineering," University of Pittsburgh, 2015. www.pitt.edu.

University of Pennsylvania. The doctors who performed the procedure were accused of having conflicts of interest because they had financial stakes in the companies that made the experimental genes. Investigators determined that these doctors tried the procedure on Gelsinger before it was proved to be safe.

Another ethical requirement—for biomedical engineers to consider the larger consequences of their work—is one of the most difficult ethical standards to monitor and enforce. For example, the same techniques that allow doctors to replace faulty genes that cause certain diseases with normal genes can also be used to create so-called designer babies for people who want "perfect" children. Questions have emerged about whether biomedical engineers should create techniques like this that can be abused for nonmedical purposes. If so, who should decide what uses are permitted and what traits are "desirable"? Should these technologies only be available to those who can pay? While no one can predict the ethical controversies that may emerge from an invention, biomedical engineers must still consider the possibilities.

CHAPTER 4

What Is It Like to Work as a Biomedical Engineer?

Biomedical engineers can work in a variety of settings for a variety of companies and institutions. As biomedical engineer Irene Bacalocostantis states, "You can work in industry, academia, and government. The doors are wide open."[28]

Biomedical Industry Work

A typical workday for a biomedical engineer who works for a company that creates and manufactures medical products varies with the job. Lori Laird, for instance, works for Guidant, which makes devices that allow doctors to clean out clogged arteries and perform other heart-related procedures without making large incisions. During her workday, she might attend a meeting with a colleague, answer e-mails, attend a class about something like preventing medical devices from becoming contaminated with bacteria, speak with a doctor about his or her request for a new device, and use a computer or drawing board to design a new device. The process of designing and developing new devices involves generating an idea that achieves a certain purpose, doing research on similar devices that may be in use, determining what materials are needed, and ensuring that the device complies with industry standards and regulations.

> "You can work in industry, academia, and government. The doors are wide open."[28]
>
> —Biomedical engineer Irene Bacalocostantis, who works for the FDA

Once a new device goes into production, Laird may spend time helping people in her company's manufacturing department determine why a glitch has developed. Once a product is built,

Some biomedical engineers go into teaching. Working with and mentoring college students can be a satisfying complement to academic research.

she visits hospitals to observe clinical trials in which it is being tested or surgeries in which it is used after it is approved. She calls watching these surgeries a high point for her; it "kind of wraps everything up and it tells you, 'This is what my job's about,' and it really makes it rewarding." Laird also supervises two technicians who help with every stage of the product development process. Her job thus involves working with a range of people. A good engineer, she notes, is "somebody that can communicate with the technician as well as the director of a project."[29]

Some jobs in industry have a more specific focus; many such engineers work only on designing, producing, testing, marketing, or teaching doctors to use a product. For Walt Baxter, who works for the Medtronic company, being a biomedical engineer involves extensive travel. Baxter develops X-ray technologies that allow doctors to monitor how implanted devices like heart pacemakers are working. He spends much of his time traveling around the world, teaching physicians how to collect certain types of X-ray images from patients so Medtronic's technologies can be applied.

A New Use for Computer Chips

A big part of working as a biomedical engineer involves reading about new advances in science and engineering and using these advances to save lives. In September 2017 biomedical engineers at the University of Illinois, Urbana-Champaign, announced that they utilized computer chip innovations to create a microfluidic chip that uses one drop of blood to test for sepsis, a serious blood infection that affects 1.5 million Americans and kills 250,000 each year. A microfluidic chip contains microscopic channels through which fluids flow so they can be analyzed.

Sepsis occurs when the immune system overreacts to a bacterial infection and produces massive quantities of immune cells and chemicals. This overwhelms the body with inflammation, broken blood vessels, and organ failure. Antibiotics can cure sepsis if given soon after the infection starts, but symptoms do not usually appear until the infection reaches dangerous levels. "The time it takes to locate and start to treat the infection is what gets sepsis patients in trouble," explains team leader Rashid Bashir. "Our strategy focuses on looking at the start of an immune response. The chip detects immune system factors mobilizing in the blood to fight the infection before the patient shows symptoms like a high fever."

Quoted in National Institute of Biomedical Imaging and Bioengineering, "Microfluidic Chip Rapidly IDs Deadly Blood Infection," September 11, 2017. www.nibib.nih.gov.

Working in a Hospital

Biomedical engineers who create products can also work in hospitals. Tom Chau is the vice president for research at the Holland Bloorview Kids Rehabilitation Hospital in Toronto, Canada. He and his colleagues create technologies that help children with severe disabilities communicate using whatever capabilities (such as blinking their eyes) they have. According to the American Institute for Medical and Biological Engineering (AIMBE), "Chau gives voices to children that have never uttered a word or taken a single step."[30] Chau's work thus involves observing and analyzing patients' capabilities, brainstorming methods of using those capabilities, and working in a laboratory to create appropriate products.

In one case, Chau's team determined that a severely disabled young adult named Jonathan could control his mouth movements. They used thermal imaging to track the ways in which Jonathan opened and closed his mouth, and they taught him to communicate using these motions. Thermal imaging cameras detect heat and can be used to detect differences in heat emission that signify movement. The team then invented computer software that translated Jonathan's mouth movements into commands that caused a computer keyboard to type whatever Jonathan wished to communicate. His first typed word was "muther." Chau noted that this was the first time Jonathan communicated with his mother, making the experience "really incredible"[31] for all involved.

Teaching and Research in Academia

Some biomedical engineers who work in hospitals or corporations also teach. Chau, for example, is a professor at the Institute of Biomaterials and Biomedical Engineering at the University of Toronto, so his days involve teaching and meeting with students as well as doing research in a hospital.

Other biomedical engineers are full-time professors and researchers. Robert Nerem, for example, has been a professor and academic researcher since 1964. He taught at Ohio State University and the University of Houston before helping establish the Bioengineering Department at Georgia Tech in 1987. His career path reflects his love of teaching and mentoring students. He says he never tires of "helping students find their passions"[32] and notes, "My greatest satisfaction professionally has come from the young people with whom I have worked and had the privilege of mentoring."[33] Nerem thus devotes much time to talking and listening to individual students, along with his teaching and research duties.

> "My greatest satisfaction professionally has come from the young people with whom I have worked and had the privilege of mentoring."[33]
>
> —Georgia Tech biomedical engineering professor Robert Nerem

A career in academia also involves behind-the-scenes activity. Professors prepare lectures for the classes they teach, and they create and assess quizzes and exams. Many professors also write textbooks that they and other professors use in classrooms. In addition, many colleges and universities require professors to serve on academic committees that determine course content and on research ethics committees that assess compliance with ethical guidelines. Professors can also volunteer as leaders in professional organizations like the Biomedical Engineering Society.

Many professors direct their own laboratory as well as doing research. Catherine Klapperich describes directing her lab at Boston University as similar to running a small business. She selects, supervises, and teaches the undergraduates, graduate students, and postdoctoral fellows who work in the lab, as well as preparing a budget and applying for research funding. Professors also write up research results and submit these reports for publication in scientific journals. Some professors present their research findings at professional conferences worldwide.

Working in Government Offices

Biomedical engineers who are employed by government regulatory agencies can work in the field, in an office, or both. Those in the field perform inspections at laboratories and manufacturing plants of companies that create and manufacture drugs or biomedical devices to ensure that these companies follow laws and policies designed to keep the public safe. Those who work in-house at agencies like the FDA determine which innovations are approved for widespread use or which products should be withdrawn from the market because of dangerous effects. For example, Richard Gray works at the FDA's Center for Devices and Radiological Health. He evaluates new cardiac devices for safety and effectiveness by studying research reports from clinical trials and recommends that the FDA either approve or not approve these devices for widespread use. Gray also does basic research on cardiac electrophysiology—the study of the electrical activity generated by the heart. He thus wears multiple "hats"

A Biomedical Engineer Who Did the Impossible

Daniel Timms had an unconventional idea for an artificial heart that could pump forever. Most artificial hearts contain numerous moving parts that quickly wear out after pumping blood 42 million times per year like a real human heart does. But Timms's invention, called the BiVACOR, has only one moving part; a spinning disk with fins that floats in a magnetic field. "The spinning part will never wear out. It never touches anything. There's no mechanical wear," explains cardiac surgeon Billy Cohn.

Most experts told Timms his idea could not work. However, several renowned heart surgeons believed in Timms and helped him procure research funding. For fifteen years Timms traveled worldwide, consulting clinicians and biomedical engineers at universities or hospitals for help with technical issues. He often slept on a couch in these experts' laboratories.

Timms hoped his invention would save his father's life, but his father died before it was ready. Timms forged on nonetheless to try to help others. In 2015 a team of surgeons and veterinarians implanted Timms's prototype into a sheep, and it worked well. Further tests are under way. Doctors believe the BiVACOR could replace the need to transplant donor hearts in the future.

Quoted in Trent Dalton, "Beating the Odds," *Australian* (Surry Hills, Australia), March 4, 2016. http://bivacor.com.

in his everyday work. His choice to do so illustrates the opportunities for biomedical engineers to customize their jobs to fit their interests and passions.

Working Hours and Pay

Biomedical engineers work full time, no matter what their specific job may be. Many work regular hours, but some must work overtime to meet certain deadlines or to fit into the schedules of doctors or others with whom they collaborate. And some who have personal reasons for relentlessly pursuing an idea work many, many overtime hours for many, many years. The Australian biomedical engineer Daniel Timms is one such person. He worked sixteen to twenty hours per day for fifteen years to bring his idea for an artificial heart to fruition because his father had heart failure, and donor hearts for transplantation are scarce.

Biomedical engineers' wages vary with the job. In 2016 the Bureau of Labor Statistics (BLS) listed $94,800 as the median annual wage for those who research and develop biomedical products; $88,810 for those in medicine manufacturing; $86,860 for those in medical equipment manufacturing; and $73,960 for those who work in laboratories in hospitals. The median wage means that half the biomedical engineers with the job earned more than the median amount and half earned less.

Among all biomedical engineers in the United States, the BLS listed the median annual wage as $85,620 in 2016. The lowest-paid 10 percent earned less than $51,050, and the highest-paid 10 percent earned more than $134,620. In comparison, the median annual pay for all occupations was $37,040, and for engineers in general was $77,900.

Geographic location also influences biomedical engineers' salary. In 2016 the states with the highest wages were Minnesota ($101,710 annual mean wage); Colorado ($101,490); New Mexico ($100,950); New York ($99,490); and California ($97,990). However, wages in some metropolitan areas surpass the state average. For example, the highest annual mean wage for biomedical engineers in the United States was $132,960 in San Jose, California. Next in line was Tucson, Arizona, with $119,410.

CHAPTER 5

Advancement and Other Job Opportunities

Biomedical engineers can advance their careers through experience and education. Earning advanced degrees and/or job promotions or transfers to other jobs can result in higher salaries for these engineers. These achievements can also elevate individuals' status within the discipline and increase their influence at a particular company or institution.

Advanced Degrees

Earning a bachelor's degree in biomedical engineering allows many people to find a job right away, but many others continue their education to earn master's or PhD degrees in biomedical engineering or related fields. Some graduates earn a master of business administration (MBA) to gain expertise in the business aspects of biomedical engineering. Others pursue advanced degrees from a medical school (MD, or doctor of medicine) or law school (JD, or doctor of law).

Typically, people with graduate degrees earn higher salaries and can advance to leadership positions within companies or academic institutions. According to Salary.com, in 2017 the median salary for a new biomedical engineer with a bachelor's degree was $50,413 to $55,224 in the United States. A midlevel job for a biomedical engineer with a master's degree and five to ten years of experience paid a median of $88,225 to $94,888. The median salary range for a senior engineer with more than fifteen years' experience and a PhD, MD, or JD was $92,140 to $102,581.

Advancement in Academia

Biomedical engineers with a PhD often become college or university professors who teach and conduct research in their own laboratories. They are often considered to be authorities in their field and may be consulted by private businesses or government agencies to serve as advisers on technical or public health policy issues. Income from consulting can add to a professor's earnings.

Biomedical engineers in academia who obtain patents for the products or techniques they invent can also earn money whenever the rights to use the patented item are sold. Actually, the university and the inventor both obtain these patents and reap the benefits. In many cases professors start their own companies to produce and sell the patented items. Some of these professors end up leaving academia because they earn far more money as entrepreneurs. But many who form companies remain in academia; some hire managers to run the company, and some work part-time at the company. For example, Dr. Kyriacos Athanasiou at the University of California–Irvine has been creating and patenting new drug delivery systems and biomaterials since the 1990s and has created several companies that license the technologies. He says he thought about leaving academia to run these companies, but "I realized that I've never been interested in creating products solely for making money. To me, it's about the excitement and passion of coming up with solutions to some of the most difficult problems that afflict humans"[34] and sharing that excitement with students. So he leaves the business aspects of his companies to managers.

> "I realized that I've never been interested in creating products solely for making money.
> To me, it's about the excitement and passion of coming up with solutions to some of the most difficult problems that afflict humans."[34]
>
> —Dr. Kyriacos Athanasiou of the University of California–Irvine

Professors who remain at a college or university for a set amount of time can also receive tenure, which provides job security, status, and often more money than untenured positions. The American Association of University Professors defines *tenure* as

Biomedical engineers who want to take on new challenges sometimes turn to academic research and teaching. More money and an enhanced reputation may result for engineers who develop new products or techniques through their research.

"an indefinite appointment that can be terminated only for cause or under extraordinary circumstances" and notes that its main purpose is "to safeguard academic freedom. . . . If faculty members can lose their positions for what they say in the classroom or for what they write in an article, they are unlikely to risk addressing controversial issues."[35] Tenure often allows professors to undertake research that may not provide immediate results, since unlike untenured professors, those with tenure cannot be fired for failing to publish a certain number of research papers each year.

Professors can also advance to lead departments or entire schools. Gilda Barabino, for instance, is the dean of the Grove School of Engineering at the City College of New York, as well as being a professor of biomedical engineering and chemical engineering. She was previously a professor of biomedical engineering and the first vice provost for academic diversity at Georgia Tech, and she is known for her advocacy and efforts to promote diversity nationwide. These efforts stemmed from obstacles she encountered as both a woman and an African American. In fact, a remark by her high school chemistry teacher in the 1970s spurred her decision to pursue a career in science. "She told the class that chemistry was not for girls," Barabino states. "I thought how dare you pick a group and say a particular subject is not acceptable for them!"[36] In 1986 Barabino became the first African American admitted to Rice University's PhD program in chemical engineering, and her expertise on diversity has made her a widely acclaimed consultant on this issue.

Other Types of Advancement

Earning a PhD can also open doors to leadership and management positions in private industry. Product engineers can become senior engineers who direct teams that create products. Alireza Rezania, PhD, is a senior scientific director at ViaCyte, where he leads a team that aims to develop a cell-based cure for type 1 diabetes. Besides providing scientific expertise, Rezania notes that his job requires him to "manage relationships with diverse collaborators in academia and industry" as well as performing "strategic planning, project leadership, laboratory and budget management, setting aggressive technical and business goals and leading diverse teams in stem cell discovery and implantable devices."[37]

Biomedical engineers in leadership positions in industry or academia can further advance their careers by transitioning to positions of authority in government agencies. Grace Peng advanced her career as an academic researcher and professor at the Catholic University of America when she became the director of research programs in mathematical modeling and computer simulation at the National Institute of Biomedical Imaging and Bioengineering (NIBIB) in 2002. As a director, she evaluates proposals from researchers, decides how research funds are spent, and determines how research is prioritized to help people with health care needs as quickly as possible. Peng also has the authority to set up committees that help government agencies promote promising research. In 2003 she set up the Interagency Modeling and Analysis Group, which consists of

"It's really a bigger picture look at science and guiding where the whole field should go. This is my niche."[38]

—Grace Peng, director of research programs in mathematical modeling and computer simulation at NIBIB representatives from ten government agencies, including the National Institutes of Health, for this purpose. She notes that she enjoys the opportunities her position gives her to support promising research and to influence the evolution of biomedical engineering in general. "It's really a bigger picture look at science and guiding where the whole field should go. This is my niche,"[38] she states.

Adding Medicine, Law, or Business to the Mix

Biomedical engineers who earn MD, JD, or MBA degrees and work as physicians, lawyers, or business managers can earn higher salaries than those with only a biomedical engineering degree. Someone who works as a physician can earn between $200,000 and $500,000 annually on average, depending on the specialty. A biomedical engineer with a law degree who works as a patent attorney can earn approximately $135,000 to $160,000 during the first year and more later on. Earning an MBA can lead to a promotion to department or division manager at a biomedical device company. In 2017 the average yearly salary for a biomedical engineering manager was $109,000.

Biomedical engineers earn additional advanced degrees for varying reasons. E.E. "Jack" Richards III worked at Prucka Engineering as a field engineer after studying biomedical engineering at Texas A&M University. The company develops electronic systems that help heart specialists diagnose heart conditions. Richards loved traveling around the world representing the products Prucka made, but after three years he found himself wondering where he would be in ten years. "I did not see myself continuing to tour the seven seas in my late thirties; I would hopefully be married with kids. I also did not see myself happy moving along the engineering, management, or sales career paths at my company,"[39] he writes. After visiting a friend who had degrees in mechanical engineering and law, Richards decided he would enjoy being a patent attorney. He completed law school, passed the Texas state bar exam and a federal patent bar exam in 2001, and began working as a patent attorney for clients who invent biomedical devices. Patent attorneys can help inventors obtain

Continuous Learning for Advancement

Earning a degree that qualifies one to work as a biomedical engineer does not mean an individual can stop learning about the constantly evolving advances in related science and engineering fields. It is important for biomedical engineers to stay current on innovations in computer technologies, biomaterials, molecular biology, bioengineering, and other specialties so these innovations can be incorporated into new biomedical inventions. This is especially important for biomedical engineers who wish to advance their careers to become managers or department leaders or who want to work in government agencies that regulate biomedical products.

Many universities have therefore introduced courses and programs to meet this need. For example, the Jacobs School of Engineering at the University of California–San Diego offers a master of advanced study degree in medical device engineering. The university's website states that this program "is designed for early to mid-career design engineers who are on a technical leadership track within their companies, or who are interested in learning the business development and regulatory issues associated with the design of novel devices and instrumentation."

University of California–San Diego, "Master of Advanced Study Degree," 2016. http://jacobsschool.ucsd.edu.

patents from the US Patent and Trademark Office or can represent companies that sue other companies for patent infringement. Either way, they must understand the technologies used in these inventions. Although Richards works long hours, he notes that he still spends a lot of time with his family. This would not have been possible had he remained on his original career path.

Curtis Neason also went back to school after working in industry. He started as a clinical engineer at Prucka Engineering, teaching cardiologists to use devices that diagnose irregular heartbeats. He was promoted to international product manager and later to global product manager. These positions involved overseeing marketing and employee training and forging partnerships and collaborations with other companies. Neason earned an MBA degree from New York University to help him understand the business and financial aspects of these jobs and found that the advanced degree gave him the expertise to merge his engineering career with his high-level management position.

CHAPTER 6

What Does the Future Hold for Biomedical Engineers?

The future looks bright for biomedical engineers. The BLS expects employment opportunities to grow by 7 percent through 2026, from 21,300 to 22,800 jobs. The BLS notes that this is "as fast as average"[40] compared to other occupations.

A Need for Subspecialists

The BLS and other agencies that track job trends believe this job growth will occur for several reasons. First, innovations in basic and applied sciences and technologies are occurring at breakneck speed, and biomedical engineers in many subspecialties can harness and apply these innovations to new biomedical products. For instance, biomedical engineers are using increasingly sophisticated 3-D printing technologies to create custom-made body organs like windpipes and bladders and biocompatible tools like stents that keep diseased arteries open.

Applying these new technologies to biomedical engineering requires an increasing number of specialized biomedical engineers who can collaborate with scientists, physicians, and other engineers. As the BLS notes, the ability of biomedical engineers "to work in different activities with workers from other fields is enlarging the range of applications for biomedical engineering products and services."[41] As the range of applications expands, the number of jobs in industry, academia, and government also grows. In addition, as biomedical advances continue, the World

Health Organization (WHO) emphasizes that there is a growing need for biomedical engineers to work with social policy experts to make these innovations accessible to people worldwide, even in areas with limited financial resources. "This in turn will require new sets of skills for biomedical engineers,"[42] and will perhaps open new job types for biomedical engineers, WHO notes.

The Aging Population

Another factor driving the increasing need for biomedical engineers is that people are living and remaining active longer. This aging population is driving a need and demand for biomedical devices and replacement parts such as artificial knees and hips, as well as artificial organs to replace worn-out or diseased organs. "In addition, as the public continues to become more aware of medical advances, increasing numbers of people will seek biomedical solutions to their health problems from their physicians,"[43] notes the BLS.

The demand for hip and knee replacements to replace painful, worn-down joints is especially prevalent; experts expect the number of hip replacements to increase by 137 percent and the number of knee replacements to increase by 607 percent by 2030. This demand has led to a need for biomedical engineers to develop new materials and tools that make these operations easier and less traumatic, with longer-lasting results. As a research paper by biomedical engineer Yuhua Li and his team at the South China University of Technology notes, "As human life span grows, the need of biomaterials will definitely continue to increase."[44]

Materials used to create replacement joints must be strong, compatible with human tissue so they do not cause inflammation or allergies, and nontoxic to body cells. These materials must also be resistant to corrosion and disintegration from body fluids and must integrate well with the surrounding bone tissue to which the surgeon attaches them. Yet even the strong metallic mixtures such as stainless steel or titanium that biomaterials experts have created are not perfect. These compounds sometimes corrode or break down from body fluids and can then release toxic chemicals that damage body organs. They can also crack or develop other damage from repeatedly supporting the person's body weight.

Biomedical engineers are thus working to improve these products, and new talent and ideas are needed to support these efforts.

Once better materials are developed, other biomedical engineers are needed to determine the best ways to manufacture the products, market them to hospitals and doctors, and teach surgeons to use them. There is thus an ongoing need for biomedical engineers with different specialties to see products through from idea to use in health care settings.

Emerging Roles for Biomedical Engineers

Biomedical engineers are improving the technologies needed for long-distance telesurgery, but there are still obstacles to overcome. One such obstacle is that telesurgery requires high-speed visual, voice, and computer data communications connections to eliminate delays after a surgeon sends commands to a distant robot. Any delays could result in botched surgeries. Thus, high-speed Internet connections are being used.

However, cybersecurity experts note that Internet-connected communications open telesurgery to hackers. In fact, in 2015 Tamara Bonaci at the University of Washington revealed that her research indicates that telesurgeries which utilize the Raven II robot are subject to cyberattacks. Bonaci is an electrical engineer who studies security issues related to emerging biomedical technologies. "Due to the open and uncontrollable nature of communication networks, it becomes easy for malicious entities to jam, disrupt, or take over the communication between a robot and a surgeon," she states. This could result in patient deaths. Even when Bonaci and her team encrypted the communications, it was still possible for hackers to interfere. This highlights the ways in which new biomedical engineering roles and subspecialties—such as biomedical engineers with expertise in cybersecurity—are emerging all the time.

Quoted in *MIT Technology Review*, "Security Experts Hack Teleoperated Surgical Robot," April 24, 2015. www.technologyreview.com.

Replacing Retirees

Another factor driving the increasing need for biomedical engineers is that a significant number of biomedical engineers in industry and academia are expected to retire by the mid-2020s, creating job openings for new engineers. Recruiting efforts to replace these teachers and researchers are ongoing at universities like Cornell, which states it launched the Faculty Renewal Sesquicentennial Challenge in 2010 "to recruit outstanding new faculty in the face of an unprecedented number of retirements expected over the next decade."[45] This initiative is being funded largely by donations from Cornell alumni who are committed to maintaining Cornell's position as a top university for biomedical engineering studies and research.

> "Medical and biological engineers today are carving out their own path . . . tackling some of the grand challenges facing the US and the world."[47]
>
> —AIMBE

The need for biomedical engineers to replace retiring engineers in academia and industry is not confined to the United States; a 2015 report by Engineers Canada predicted that Canada would experience a shortage of one hundred thousand engineers of all types between 2015 and 2025. In March 2017 an article in the University of Toronto Engineering Department newsletter noted that "across the country, thousands of engineers with decades of experience are about to retire *en masse* [as a group]"[46] and called on universities to train highly qualified engineers, including biomedical engineers, to fill these vacancies.

Forging the Direction of Biomedical Engineering

The newness of biomedical engineering as a formal discipline is also driving the need for new people. According to the American Institute for Medical and Biological Engineering (AIMBE), "Medical and biological engineers today are carving out their own path." The discipline has continued to evolve since it became a recognized branch of engineering in the twentieth century. This path, states AIMBE, involves "tackling some of the grand challenges facing the US and the world,"[47] and therefore it requires solutions that integrate innovations in biomaterials, computers, cell engineering, gene engineering, drug design, biomechanics, nanotechnologies, medical imaging, and more. As biomedical engineers devise new ways of using discoveries in these diverse subfields, they create new subfields that need people with new combinations of expertise.

An example of an expanding subfield is telesurgery— long-distance surgery—that allows surgeons in one place to perform surgery on a patient in a distant location by remotely controlling a surgical robot. Telesurgery is still experimental, but clinical doctors and biomedical engineers with computer expertise are developing ways to make it feasible for widespread use. This would allow surgeons to operate on patients in developing countries that have few doctors, among other uses. One additional use proposed by NASA is for telesurgery technologies to someday provide long-distance medical care to astronauts and others who travel into space.

> "The journey into the Biotech [twenty-first] Century will take us into new and exciting territory in many ways unknown but offering enormous challenges and opportunities. It is there for our taking."[48]
>
> —Biomedical engineering professor Robert Nerem of Georgia Tech

As the field of telesurgery develops, biomedical engineers with expertise in robotics, machine learning, computer programming, computer science, and telecommunications technologies will be needed to overcome limitations found in current experimental telesurgery procedures. For example, current procedures rely on doctors at the receiving end to be present in case something unexpected happens and a human is needed to take over the surgery. Some experts believe that developing surgical robots that can learn to respond to emergencies may someday make it possible for fewer doctors to participate. This would be especially valuable for people deployed on spaceships or in distant space colonies where medical personnel are scarce.

The twenty-first century is often referred to as the "Biotech Century," and in 1997 biomedical engineering pioneer Robert Nerem wrote, "The journey into the Biotech Century will take us into new and exciting territory in many ways unknown but offering enormous challenges and opportunities. It is there for our taking."[48] Thus far, unprecedented biomedical and biotech innovations are indeed presenting these opportunities and challenges, and the encouragement Nerem's prediction offered to existing and prospective biomedical engineers is as valid during the second decade of the twenty-first century as it was at the time.

CHAPTER 7

Interview with a Biomedical Engineer

Robert Langer is an institute professor of biological engineering at MIT, where he has taught and done research since 1978, after earning degrees in chemical engineering from Cornell University and MIT. Langer's laboratory at MIT is the largest biomedical engineering laboratory in the world, and he is well known as a biomedical engineering pioneer whose research on drug delivery methods, tissue engineering, biomaterials, biomechanics, and molecular engineering has largely shaped modern progress in these areas. He has written over fourteen hundred research articles and obtained more than one thousand patents. He has also received more than 220 major scientific awards and has founded many biotechnology companies. He spoke with the author about his career.

Q: Why did you become a biomedical engineer?

A: I became an engineer because I was good at math and science. I became a biomedical engineer because I was looking for a way to use my engineering background to help people. Most people who earned chemical engineering degrees in the 1970s went to work for oil companies, but I wanted to do something that would help people more. I received twenty job offers from oil companies like Shell, Chevron, and Exxon, but I wasn't excited about working for an oil company. I wanted to use engineering to make the world a better, healthier place. I was turned down for the teaching and research jobs I applied for, but finally Dr. Judah Folkman offered me a low-paying job in his laboratory at Boston Children's Hospital doing research to stop cancer by preventing it from growing a blood supply. I was the only engineer there, but I loved the work.

Q: Can you describe your typical workday?

A: My workdays are filled with teaching; meetings with students, researchers, entrepreneurs, and colleagues; speaking sometimes with media representatives; preparing and delivering lectures to students and others; writing and revising research reports; reading e-mails; writing or reviewing research grant applications; and more. Some days, I travel to various places to present research papers or to receive an award. Starting and ending each day with a workout in my home gym helps me balance my life and stay healthy and able to eat what I like—such as chocolate. I also depend heavily on six full-time administrators who manage my office and laboratory—including all the students, postdocs, and visiting scientists—juggle and print out my schedule each day, and help with some of the background work like preparing notes for lectures.

Each day is different. On one particular day, I met with an undergraduate student who sought my advice about whether to accept an industry job or go to graduate school; met with another undergraduate student who sought advice on a research project; and met with one of my former postdoctoral researchers who asked my advice on how to attract investors to a new biotech company. Then I delivered a lecture to undergraduate students, participated in a televised interview, and hosted a pizza get-together for the new undergraduate students working in my laboratory. It's important for me to get to know my students and for them to understand that I am happy to help them any way I can. I also reviewed a number of grant applications, acted as editor for a paper, and answered some hundred-plus e-mails.

Q: What do you like most about your job?

A: Coming up with ideas and working with students. I like helping students see how their ideas can change the world. And I like knowing that my work is helping people. I am proud that many of my former students and postdocs are now professors at universities all over the world and lead academic laboratories of their own. My main wish is to do good in the world, and these people are all helping to make the world a better place.

Q: What do you like least about your job?
A: Sitting on committees and writing grants.

Q: What personal qualities do you find most valuable for this type of work?
A: Creativity, because you want to come to the field with new ideas. Perseverance, because the road to completion is long. Very often things won't go well, and you have to hang in there and keep trying. And compassion, because you deal with young people (students) if you are a professor like me. I have had many failures, and at first people did not believe in my ideas. They didn't believe a chemical engineer could improve human health and figure out ways of stopping diseases like cancer. But I worked hard and didn't give up, and I try to help students realize that if you persist and do what you love doing, you can learn from those failures and succeed.

Q: What is the best way to prepare for this type of engineering job?
A: Get a great education and learn engineering and biology fundamentals. And follow your heart and do things you are passionate about. Learning the fundamentals will give you the tools you need to ask important questions and conduct innovative research. Students who ask good questions are the ones who become great.

Q: What other advice do you have for students who might be interested in a career as a biomedical engineer?
A: Dream big dreams that can change the world and don't give up when obstacles come your way. Don't be afraid to take chances and to explore ideas that others may call impossible.

Q: What do you think have been the most significant changes related to job opportunities in the field of biomedical engineering since it became a recognized branch of engineering?

A: I think it used to be more mechanical and deal with objects. Now it's getting more molecular and sometimes deals with small technologies like nanotechnologies. These changes mean biomedical engineers must educate themselves about more and different subfields so they can put together engineering and medicine to come up with new ideas.

SOURCE NOTES

Introduction: A Growing Engineering Field

1. International Federation of Consulting Engineers, "What Is an Engineer?" http://fidic.org.
2. Try Engineering, "What Can I Do with an Engineering Degree?," 2018. http://tryengineering.org.
3. National Human Genome Research Institute, "Biomedical Engineer." www.genome.gov.

Chapter 1: What Does a Biomedical Engineer Do?

4. American Institute for Medical and Biological Engineering, "Navigate the Circuit." http://navigate.aimbe.org.
5. Michael Sivak, "Gastrointestinal Endoscopy: Past and Future," *Gut*, August 2006, p. 1062.
6. University of Wisconsin–Madison, "Tapping the 'Wild Collaboration' Within Biomedical Engineers," February 8, 2017. www.engr.wisc.edu.
7. Quoted in Ellen Crown, "First 'Thought-Controlled' Bionic Leg Funded Through Army Medicine Research," US Army, September 26, 2013. www.army.mil.
8. Quoted in Katharine Miller, "Profiles in Computer Science Courage," *Biomedical Computation Review*, Spring 2011. www.biomedicalcomputationreview.org.

Chapter 2: How Do You Become a Biomedical Engineer?

9. Quoted in US Naval Academy, "Top 5 Reasons to Attend Summer STEM." www.usna.edu.
10. Quoted in W. Mark Saltzman, *Biomedical Engineering*. Cambridge: Cambridge University Press, 2015, p. 618.
11. Gage Greening, "Inside a NASA Internship: Gage Greening Reports from the Johnson Space Center," University of Arkansas Biomedical Engineering department blog, August 1, 2016. https://bmeblog.uark.edu.
12. Penn State Department of Agricultural and Biological Engineering, "Biological Engineering Major," 2018. www.abe.psu.edu.

13. Penn State Biomedical Engineering Department, "About the Department." www.bioe.psu.edu.
14. Saltzman, *Biomedical Engineering*, p. xv.
15. Accreditation Board for Engineering and Technology, "Why ABET Accreditation Matters." www.abet.org.
16. Lina Nilsson, "How to Attract Female Engineers," *New York Times*, April 27, 2015. www.nytimes.com.
17. Quoted in Try Engineering, "Lori Laird," 2018. http://tryengineering.org.

Chapter 3: What Skills and Personal Qualities Matter Most, and Why?

18. Try Engineering, "What Is an Engineer?," 2018. http://tryengineering.org.
19. Robert Nerem, "The Emergence of Bioengineering," *Bridge*, Winter 1997. www.nae.edu.
20. Quoted in American Institute for Medical and Biological Engineering, "Robert Langer." http://navigate.aimbe.org.
21. Quoted in Kristie Nybo, "Profile of Robert Langer," *BioTechniques*, November 2012, p. 273.
22. Quoted in Saltzman, *Biomedical Engineering*, p. 660.
23. Indiana University–Purdue University Indianapolis, "Is Biomedical Engineering Right for Me?," 2017. www.engr.iupui.edu.
24. Quoted in Try Engineering, "Lori Laird."
25. Quoted in American Institute for Medical and Biological Engineering, "Tom Chau." http://navigate.aimbe.org.
26. Biomedical Engineering Society, "Biomedical Engineering Society Code of Ethics," 2004. www.bmes.org.
27. Josephine Johnston, "Conflict of Interest in Biomedical Research," Hastings Center. www.thehastingscenter.org.

Chapter 4: What Is It Like to Work as a Biomedical Engineer?

28. Quoted in American Institute for Medical and Biological Engineering, "Irene Bacalocostantis." http://navigate.aimbe.org.
29. Quoted in Sloan Career Cornerstone Center, "Lori Laird." http://tryengineering.org.

30. American Institute for Medical and Biological Engineering, "Tom Chau."
31. Quoted in American Institute for Medical and Biological Engineering, "Tom Chau."
32. Quoted in American Institute for Medical and Biological Engineering, "Robert M. Nerem." http://navigate.aimbe.org.
33. Quoted in National Academy of Engineering, "2008 Founders Award Recipient Remarks," 2017. www.nae.edu.

Chapter 5: Advancement and Other Job Opportunities

34. Quoted in Brian Bell, "Joint Venturer," *UCI News*, October 10, 2017. https://news.uci.edu.
35. American Association of University Professors, "Tenure." www.aaup.org.
36. Quoted in Jenisha Watts, "Gilda Barabino Making Science More Inclusive," *Member Spotlight* (blog), American Association for the Advancement of Science, June 24, 2011. www.aaas.org.
37. Alireza Rezania's LinkedIn page, 2018. www.linkedin.com.
38. Quoted in American Institute for Medical and Biological Engineering, "Grace Peng." http://navigate.aimbe.org.
39. Quoted in Saltzman, *Biomedical Engineering*, p. 219.

Chapter 6: What Does the Future Hold for Biomedical Engineers?

40. Bureau of Labor Statistics, US Department of Labor, *Occupational Outlook Handbook*, "Biomedical Engineers," October 24, 2017. www.bls.gov.
41. Bureau of Labor Statistics, US Department of Labor, *Occupational Outlook Handbook*, "Biomedical Engineers."
42. World Health Organization, "Human Resources for Medical Devices, the Role of Biomedical Engineers," 2017. http://apps.who.int.
43. Bureau of Labor Statistics, US Department of Labor, *Occupational Outlook Handbook*, "Biomedical Engineers."
44. Yuhua Li et al., "New Developments of Ti-Based Alloys for Biomedical Application," *Materials*, March 4, 2014. www.mdpi.com.

45. Cornell University, "Stephen T. Mong Commits $500K Gift to BME for Faculty Renewal," *Cornell Engineering Newsletter*, September 2015. www.bme.cornell.edu.
46. Cristina Amon et al., "The Engineers Who Built Everything Are Retiring. Canada Needs Highly Qualified Graduates to Replace Them," *University of Toronto Engineering News*, March 16, 2017. http://news.engineering.utoronto.ca.
47. American Institute for Medical and Biological Engineering, "History." http://navigate.aimbe.org.
48. Nerem, "The Emergence of Bioengineering."

FIND OUT MORE

Accreditation Board for Engineering and Technology (ABET)

415 N. Charles St.
Baltimore, MD 21201
www.abet.org

ABET is a nonprofit organization that accredits college and university programs that grant associate's, bachelor's, and master's degrees in natural and applied sciences, engineering, engineering technologies, and computers. The website contains a list of programs ABET accredits and also has information about the purpose and standards for accreditation.

American Institute for Medical and Biological Engineering (AIMBE)

1400 Eye St. NW, Suite 235
Washington, DC 20005
http://aimbe.org

AIMBE is a nonprofit organization that represents medical and biological engineers and related academic institutions, private industries, and professional engineering societies in advocating for relevant public policy issues. The AIMBE website contains articles that highlight biomedical advances and careers and provides guidance for students interested in these careers.

Biomedical Engineering Society (BMES)

8201 Corporate Dr., Suite 1125
Landover, MD 20785
www.bmes.org

The BMES is a professional society for biomedical engineers and bioengineers. It promotes education and shares knowledge about biomedical engineering with the public. The BMES allows undergraduate and graduate students studying biomedical engineering to join as student members and have access to meetings, workshops, and other resources.

National Institute of Biomedical Imaging and Bioengineering (NIBIB)

9000 Rockville Pike
Building 31, Room 1C14
Bethesda, MD 20892
www.nibib.nih.gov

NIBIB is a government agency within the National Institutes of Health that performs, promotes, and funds biomedical research. The NIBIB website contains information about biomedical engineering careers. NIBIB has created an interactive game called "Want to Be a Bioengineer?" for middle and high school students interested in biomedical engineering careers. It can be found at: www.nibib.nih.gov/science-education.

National Society of Professional Engineers (NSPE)

1420 King St.
Alexandria, VA 22314
www.nspe.org

NSPE is a professional organization for engineers. Its website contains information about what various types of engineers— including biomedical engineers—do and discusses professional ethics and other issues that affect engineers.

Try Engineering

http://tryengineering.org

Try Engineering is an online resource that provides extensive information about engineering careers. It includes interviews with working engineers, hands-on activities, and links to engineering programs at colleges and universities and information about summer programs and internships.

INDEX

PICTURE CREDITS

ABOUT THE AUTHOR

Melissa Abramovitz is an award-winning author/freelance writer who specializes in writing educational nonfiction books and magazine articles for all age groups, from preschoolers through adults. She has published hundreds of magazine articles and more than fifty educational books for children and teenagers. She also writes short stories, poems, and picture books and is the author of an acclaimed book for writers. Melissa graduated summa cum laude from the University of California–San Diego with a degree in psychology and is also a graduate of the Institute of Children's Literature.